FRACTURED

Danny Baker

Punk ★ Hostage ★ Press

FRACTURED
Danny Baker

ISBN 978-0-9851293-0-9
© 2012 Punk Hostage Press

Punk Hostage Press
P.O. Box 1869
Hollywood, CA 90078
www.punkhostagepress.com

Editor:
A. Razor

Associate Editor:
Iris Berry

Cover Design:
Billy Burgos

Printed by 1984 Printing, Oakland, CA, USA
on 100% recycled pcw, acid free paper
www.1984printing.com

Editor's Acknowledgments

This is an expanded version of a chapbook that was published on December 2, 2011.
The chapbook was made to accompany the first public reading of the author's work at Beyond Baroque Literary/Arts Center in Venice Beach, CA.

Danny Baker did an impressive job that night at the reading. In the days before the reading, Rafael and Melissa Alvarado, Billy Burgos and Danny all worked together on getting the chapbook together in time for the reading. This book was inspired by their efforts and has been edited by myself to include more work from Danny Baker than the original chapbook and also to be the initial offering from this new and powerful writer.
It has also become Iris Berry's, as well as my own, first choice as the inaugural offering for our new publishing concern, Punk Hostage Press.

I would like to thank all those who made that night possible, as well as the chapbook that has made this collection of poems possible.

Richard Modiano, Dennis and Annette Cruz, S.A. Griffin, Rafael and Melissa Alvarado and most notably, Billy Burgos for the original cover design and artwork that we tried to remain true to. Also, so importantly, the audience of friends and supporters who were there to share that evening with us all.

Thank you, posthumously, as well, to Scott Wannberg and Mike Taylor, who encouraged Danny Baker to write and publish more in the last year or so of their lives.

Last, but not least, thanks goes out to Danny Baker for allowing us to make his words the first offering of our humble press as we begin to renew our spirit of providing words and books to those that want and need them.

And, of course, special thanks to all of the readers of Danny Baker who have inspired, promoted and supported him and his work into the stature of a writer that he is at today. May you find this collection as fulfilling to read as it was to work on for us.

A. Razor 2012

Introduction

In the early part of the 1980's Danny Baker, A. Razor and myself ran the same streets reckless. Crossing paths on and around an abandoned Hollywood Boulevard, where people came, once upon a time, following tabloid promises of fame and fortune. By the time we arrived, all that was left were the picked over and the forgotten, pushing shopping carts, selling incense and sleeping in doorways, still waiting for their close-ups. We were searching for others like ourselves, running from homes where we were no longer welcome. Frequenting the same bars, nightclubs and newsstands. Arrested by the same cops and on a first name basis with all the same homeless people, drug dealers, hookers, bartenders and doormen. We listened to the same bands and hung out and slept at the same crash pads. We had our way with Hollywood Boulevard and Hollywood Boulevard had its way with us. Meeting Danny Baker at that point in time, was apparently not in the cards.

It was only a year and a half ago in August of 2010, when A. Razor and I did meet Danny Baker, and it was nowhere near Hollywood Boulevard. He talked about writing, asking a million questions, and to both our surprise, he was really listening. He wanted to know. He wanted to know because deep inside of him was an amazing and gifted, twisted and talented, voracious and prolific writer, aching to burst out. Never have I seen someone so determined to do what he was really meant to be doing, do an about-face and then show us all just how it's done. Awe inspiring and painfully articulate. Danny Baker has arrived and he is not going anywhere, there's plenty more where this came from. This book of poems is a result of Danny's unimaginable journey from Hollywood Boulevard to Wall Street and then to the Hawaiian Islands, only to realize that he left his soul on Hollywood Boulevard. Fractured is a rough ride through Danny Baker's eyes, ears, heart, soul and psyche, a much needed new voice that will give you answers to questions you didn't know you had, inspire you, scare you, break your heart and leave you wanting more. I promise... - Iris Berry 2012

Dedication

I'd like to dedicate this work to Iris Berry and A. Razor. One could not ask for better mentors. Their friendship has lifted me to new heights and helped open a magnificent chapter in life; that of the word, upon whose wings I attempt to soar. I am eternally grateful, Iris and Razor. Thank you.

I also offer my thanks to Rafael & Melissa Alvarado and Billy Burgos for their assistance in arranging my debut reading and original chap.

To my sister Cindy; always looking out when nobody else would. And to mom, we've come a long way. I love you.

To my girl DL, how the fuck you put up with me, I have no clue, but thank you from the bottom of my heart…infinity baby…and a thousand gerber daisies in each of your dreams.

Adam, Scotty, Davey, Doc Scott, thanks for keeping me sane (clearly a relative term) and out of prison… A few good friends is more than most will ever see. Each of you has gone out of your way to render me quite rich in that arena. There is a large contingent I have failed to mention. I think you know who you are. I hope you do and apologize for all that I've left out.

Finally, I have not traversed these lands alone. To those who paved the meandering path of the word, to friends and enemies alike, living and not, who have provided never ending inspiration, critique and simple readership of and for my work, to them I owe a tremendous bow of respect. Excluding enemies (they're not worth the ink) and with the knowledge that I would forget many were I to attempt to list all those with whom I've had positive interaction, I will just extend a special hand to Carolyn Srygley Moore, Diana Rose, Mark Hartenbach and S.A Griffin for believing in me enough to encourage and 'endorse', for lack of a better term, my efforts. I am truly humbled.

To all those unmentioned, strike it up to my failing synapses, but thank you.

RIP Scott Wannberg
RIP Mike Taylor

Pieces

Note to Self 1
The Great Anarchic Train Robbery 2
Corroded Eroded and Tired 5
Before 6
Spinnin' on Tuesday 8
Sleepless 10
Electric Tape 12
What I Do 14
Half-Sensical Rambling Off The Wall of Toughness Learned 16
Thud 23
Fire 26
Escape from DC; A Semi Lucid Fractured Rant on Fracture ...29
Lotsa Luck 32
Oneloa 34
She Falls Silent When Most Sentient 35
Spilled Milk 37
Another Lessoned Learned 40
They Only Have Eyes For Two 43
Mercy Killing 45
Dead Stars Are Heavy 46
Country Bear Jamboree Growl 49
How Many Boulders To The Margins 51
Six Ways to Sunday 52
A Stroll Down Sentiment Row 54
My Brain Crashed Into Two Poems & Can't Get Up 56
Ain't Nothing Sacred Anymore 58
Day Dreaming Away (For A. Razor) 60
Time To Smoke This Joint, Smokey (For Scott Wannberg) 62
Skid Row L.A. 66
playing like Copeland when moon is called for 69
A Matter of Price 71
Assorted Contemplations of a Stranger in a Strange Animal Farm 73
Blurring Lines in the Abstract of a Linear Mind 75
Dark 76

On the Tip of Tongue Yet Inarticulable 77
Deviant New Normal of the So Called All-Inclusive 79
Outcast 81
Dorothy & Toto 83
Fog 88
Hopped On A Bus 90
Depraved Reflection 92
Rent a Cop High Wire Near Miss 93
Odaratio Suetes 95
Rage 96
Disconnected 97
Sunset Dance With Buddy Guy & Suicidal Tendencies 98
One Way Out 99
Red Pool 101
Personality 103
On an Unlit Street 104
Seeking What's Lost Where I fear No Evil 106
One Choice 107
Slow Drain 109
Solitaire 110
The Last of The New Mohicans 112
Stone Grumblings from a Rock in the Pacific 115
Time's Changing 5 118
seizure 120
Do They Know 122

Note to Self

deeper and deeper
breathless
laughing or weeping
fuming at insensitivity
who gives a fuck
punch 'em in the side of the head
don't ask if it's good enough
it never is
so shut the fuck up
excavate
open oily ink veins
slide through the bowels of
the wrong side
of track marked streets
walk 'em into the
gutter of the bondage section
of your porn shop mind
crap on the floor
of societal expectation
blow a wad on tradition
make them gasp and sigh and pray
      for you
            and your lost soul
piss on all they hold holy
kick yourself in the nuts
bleed like Darby
if you can't make 'em cry your tears
make them laugh your nonsense

The Great Anarchic Train Robbery

nowhere to go but deeper in ancient fantasy
stomping wild through the streets with no sanctuary, only a
step back into abysmal jaw of death incarnate
as a world explores revolt as if it were first to land on
subversive shores despite word found in
dusty tomes rarely opened in sections of the library
declared off limits by the masses of salvation

lessons not limited to binary era
are no longer relevant apparently and as
human nature hasn't changed since the start
that which tackles such issues as Holland tulip bulb bubbles,
empirical sagacious warning a hundred years before a lone
  fiddler fiddled
in glow of death of a city burning under the weight of its
  collective immorality,
and shuffled deck chairs on a ship doomed by fallacy and
  inattention to knowledge
stand one and all, unwelcome, in mono-rhetorical voice of
  progressive mutiny, facts
uncovered from careful concealment only serve to capsize ships
  already listing,
discover land already discovered but obfuscated in convenient
  desert storms
of popular acrimony misplaced and palpably ineffectual in
  achieving goal
as stated, for as stated they violate principles of existence existing
long before MTV rocked votes to the left
before churches hymned to the right
prior to digital attention span

nowhere to go but deeper in ancient fantasy
sleeping tranquil over rambunctious streets despite
  circumstances
less than ideal for a lone young traveler

traipsing boulevards of past glory upon which he likely did not
   belong
but for heaving convulsions speaking
volumes of alternative housing arrangements more repugnant
   than
grime slime stairwells of malodorous air

elitists who would beg to differ
erase etchings on walls, silencing echoes
that don't serve its intent whatever intent it may be
at that moment in time when pendulum over-shoots its arc
sending ants into a furious search for scapegoats to encumber
   though
finding vertigo when forced to look through clear lens into the
   dark mirror
that always stares back sending shock waves of revulsion
   through the sentient
while leaving the unfortunate dim numb out of some misguided
   recompense for
ill-conceived plan to level a playing field that hasn't been level
   since creation
as that's just the way the genes fly and truth is the numb are
   happier than
those of superlative cognition anyway, introspectives left
   melancholy
watching in saddened bemusement the death of liberty
at the very hands of those who would so protest
as they vote for more regulation to ironically
render themselves more free

nowhere to go but deeper in ancient fantasy
retreating to the warmth of word
on a rooftop above the fray as ants scurry below
and 25 seems like a proper age
to shoot for if lucky and anything more seems
just a pipe dream resembling
something closer to a nightmare on loop

as the pendulum has over-swung its arc
as we've overspent our means, work ethic
no longer implies effort, carefully chosen history
is selectively buried by whomever's selected, Cicero rolls
in his unheralded grave while Nero takes on Charlie Daniels
and Rome burns unimpeded under watchful eyes of a ship
   captain
incapable of winning a staring contest with an alabaster disaster
   looming
for passengers taking in what they want when they want it,
   ultimately paying
the ultimate price for their avarice, sloth and trust in humanity-
   always
suspect- for fear and greed rule all, however that's been redacted
   too
rats are jumping ship, stealing all life-boats as the ants imbibe
on a Buffet of ass served up with $40 billion of arrogance
rolling up on a jet escorted by copious security
just in time for the anointment of an oracle
perfectly manicured with a filthy agenda

 nowhere to go but deeper in ancient fantasy
digging up letters that make words
that make sentences that make paragraphs
seeking truth through the fiction
brought to you by your government and
its cronies, all of whom are here
for no reason other than to provide help

yeah

Corroded Eroded and Tired

fine grain sands meld with salt tear
over paper too thin
combustible etchings burn through

a scream into the wind is met with silence
'fore a wry retort
soaks the down-breeze in corrosive vitriol

clickety clack a roller coaster reaches apex
from precipice, only one answer
the arrows point down

stomach firmly implanted in unreceptive throat
cognizance binds to stomach
a pool of acidic bile

a trough typically of some relief
soothes not, there is no elixir
to return organs their rightful homes

it just all gets harder and harder
feeds upon itself
becomes yet more intractable

climbing to the zenith again holds no interest
acrophobia has taken a seat inside
peering over the acme, my paper crumbles

a drop of blood drips from eye
all functions askew, vitriol had its way
I drown in it, I own it

Before

trying to write hopeful listening to Leonard Cohen is
akin to watching a road through rear view reflection
notwithstanding such visceral perception
in minor key embrace is
a familiar echo of great discomfort
yet turning a deaf ear is
out of the question despite it being the only question of
ample substance

attempting to mine peace in shadow and echo seems
lacking intellectual integrity

however nothing argues with unknown
and dies bloody in its boots
hence mind eye trains to the quantified rear
of footprint already known
track still to be left presents unneeded angst

I suppose that not yet recognized
was once upon a time a carpeted field
of rolling Kentucky Blue Grass dreamscape

once upon a time, ages yore
before hope became a four letter word to conflicted soul
when kites flew beyond sight

before George Harrison's guitar gently wept on my soaking feet

before George Jones put the bottle on the table
for just one more and then another

before I met the devil at the crossroads
selling myself into purgatory
whose ends are known only to the fates;
I've yet to meet one I trust

before Manson started making sense
somehow seeming more sane
than preconditioned preconceived notions
armed with finely sharpened scythes
facing off daily were I to grant them access
via eyes lost in hills no longer green

scanning the distance for fresh pasture while
casting firebombs into every foxhole
refusing to ever again get jumped by the future

Spinnin' on Tuesday

a mobile dangles deconstructed logic over my crib
dislocated building blocks strike like Nolan Ryan heat
warpspeed wrecking ball blows fissure cranial bone

grand design demands reconstruction despite arthritic hand
former bounty of requisite sewing kit and desire to obtain one
  up and ran
everything will die though some traits need go sooner

children question all as the term itself implies
ignorance of physics of mass weight and motion killed the cat
popular misconception jailed curiosity instead

insatiable greed for mystical reply to domain of science fills pews
blood wrists blossom at obstinate existential need for logic in
  face of emotional break
riddle wrapped in enigma knocks at my door relentlessly

draining my sea of wonder its primary objective
 primary objective is the torch bearer for all that make the gods
  laugh
   although spiteful motive seems to get a kinder view from
Olympian overlords
donning transparent halos atop brooding soulful eyes they fool
  no one
though barred doors do little to keep creeps from finding cracks
an angel loses its wings with each security breech

salt and pepper ash of the fallen rests on fresh snow
heart loses a piece of peace via ingestion of noxious excretion
unlit pathways blot landscape not to be seen but felt

not up to task presents itself as most logical way out
fires of Texas heat swim the spinal canal to the real magnum
admission remains full though discharge can't keep up

spin mobile spin

Sleepless

gusts of wind blow past at warp speed
feeling pubescent looking for a bit of mayhem

finding Vonnegut & Van Gogh & Kubrick instead
sheets of wind like paper thin glass break against haoley skin

my droogs are barking like war dogs
better find a war

they tend to turn inward when lacking
foreign enemies

green tar shoulders pass as blur
sugar cane smoke stack unleashes putrid air

half a roach smells of roses
juxtaposed against such olfactory abomination

wind vines wrap their way around optics
spectacles not designed to fend off angry ocean breath

distant stars stay so
laughing at my hijinks

knowing I'll never catch 'em
nor their distant cousin, amber moon

egotists one and all
my scope trains on simplicity

I'll shoot rapids but stars are a funny bunch
think I ought to let them be for another conqueror

hope meets a mangled undignified death

I've died 12 by my count, three more than this cat's quota

Ludwig von hits me in the form of a punk rock ax
looking for another's tree to fall; my garden a hewn heap

it's never fun and games til the paramedics get called
a trailer hitch approaches at 90mph

searching for a night of ultra-violence
finding no deserving targets, nothing new anyway

just the same old introspective typist
with mild larceny in his heart
and a wake sleep cycle
aptly defined only
as fucking
insane

Electrical Tape

a circuit breaker on acid
on a perpetual loop
sequentially tripping out
to then reconnect

something a bit of electrical tape should fix

a battery ground wire
of fraying contact
playing tag with its host

something a bit of electrical tape should fix

a lamp flickers in the corner of a room
its cord, a fire in the making
beneath a well traversed Persian rug

mid-range speakers start spitting a hiss
a coffee brewer stops brewing
irons cease to iron
vacuum's cough

everything's gone on strike
worry not
a bit of magic tape will
do a trick

neurotransmitters
jump synapses or simply
transmit elsewhere
if signaling at all anymore

there's special electrical tape
for this too

I just can't find MacGyver
my bubblegum is all sugar-free and
will not adhere to the plan

and the tape,
the tape's wrapped me
in a web of which I am unable
to escape no matter how hard I try
as it sticks to me and forgets the plan too

What I Do

train rolls all night long further infuriating
sandman unstable when denied his quarry

infinite indications indicate infinite solutions
solving nothing worth effort but it's what I do

running a gauntlet of antipodal dynamic renders
exhaustion of gauntlets antipodes and dynamics

rampaging ruminations wax entropic
where the wicked gets not ample rest

resources mined to their core lam it
beckoning questions of what's next

a midnight train to Georgia departs at midday
guaranteeing no shelter from pursuing echoes

broken winged bird flops to makeshift shelter
knowing it's only a matter of time before end

inconsequential queries uncouth one and all take numbers
finding patience is a virtue none possess and punch it out

unilateral dogmatic sunday tv pundits talk over themselves
leaving me incapable of discerning whose nonsense I hear

though little is of less consequence than solving that equation
it's probable this dropout takes more than a college crack at it

a growing melee is raging in the waiting room
catapulting any plans for any geometric proof

inanity infused kool-aid overflows from a barren pantry
  cupboard

unrepentantly demanding immediate attention with each tip of
  cup

angelic departures are grounded by order of overwhelmed
powers that be unsure of how to sate dehydrated drunkards

twisted and tied in a pervasive liana of acute dissonance
running from aromatic rose petal in deference to thorns

a monster grows ever more acrimoniously distant
not proud just cognizant of facts presented clearly

Half-Sensical Rambling Off The Wall of Toughness Learned

In action
and in deed
my being wrote checks
my ass couldn't cash

Or wouldn't
yet

Floating 'cross lines
my type was just not
intended to dance
only from ultimate weakness
rose hyper-apt strength

Battles worthy un-fought
eviscerate soul
tattoo fractured heart

Until

A day comes
skies part a wide path
lightening strikes

Schoolyard bullies shrink
to not as eventually
playgrounds make way
replaced by harsh reality

Too many un-cashed checks
get cashed
close calls ringing warning bells
stop ringing
leaving flanks open to assault

Only bells now
blare from an ambulance
or patrol car

Put up or shut up
pays multiple visits

Walking no longer an option
defeat smells of fish,
a relative visiting too long

Put up or shut up
talks again

Broken bones heal far more readily than
fractured pride

A monkey called Nurture for lack of a more fitting moniker
wouldn't get the fuck off my back

I set us both aflame
Nurture didn't make it
fuck the fucking monkeys anyway

Tough enough of
amply thick skin at this point
still a bit touchy
admittedly

A survivor shines in armor
fit for the round table
prepares for fresh battle

Until

Conflict anew arrives with chest out
self inflicted as always

he coughs out yet another new conflict   as the name implies

Renders crippling impotence
turning inward upon itself with a scythe
long thought to have been buried

The wheels on the bus go round and round, round and round…
…or so the pattern seems to emerge

Reared in four terrifying walls
sent to playgrounds unwelcoming

From playgrounds
to urban campgrounds less welcoming

The hills to the streets
and back to the hill via The Street
which immediately takes up arms in protest
begins a dream-shatter campaign

For only degrees need apply yet somehow
I made it past the initial selection
though finding peace in that fact is elusive
as sands dripped through digits
of gilded empire lost, humanity not found
and the final cut is sharp as hell

Heart went on a sabbatical in grey pinstripe
though blue was really the power color of the time
always close but never quite on the mark

Experience levels smarts
like gentrification
to character of community

We had lunch the other day,
experience and I

talked of what we've shared
all these years

He reminded me
I left some checks un-cashed
in my younger days
I nodded to the affirmative
before explaining
how it all works for me now

I cash every fucking one
and a few I never wrote
just to balance books
left listing in wake
of those I missed

A childhood spent
pondering and on the run

Life happened, I went on,
I learned true fear
life and limb just do not
enter the picture

Fear lingers
I don't like fear
call it angst instead

Experience was confounded
as to how life and limb could be
excluded from talk of fear
In time, I told him
life would happen to him as well
awakening his senses
to pain, real pain the likes of which
no weapon could replicate

He would stare dead
into death's eye
shouting "I don't give a fuck!"
while ripping it
from it's ocular socket...
...or not

But, I advised
the latter choice would be so unwise

Orthopedic bills are cheaper than those of psychiatrists
I surmised

With internalized discord
oft perceived as weakness, comes
invincibility of soul

Only in setting life and limb
out on their own, does
the caged beast free himself
where so required

From the fire-pit, rises the phoenix

Experience and I said our goodbyes
he went to get more

Incessant warring factions
fractionalize, though
actually scare me at times

In the end however,
I've paid off mine

See me if yours has been
put on hold for some odd reason

Resubmit it- you may get lucky
though think twice, NSF isn't a stamp
used by my bankers ever since I
sent concern for anatomical pain packing
quite a number of years back
Just plain ugly toughened now
never invincible
but for the fact I don't care
about that fact

Tough enough
is back in the kitchen
getting added time with the oven

I can't help but chuckle
thinking of soul forever lost
in fear of trivial pain
when the real thing walked
in my door at birth

Trivial pursuits   *pursued*
in deference to viscous blood
eschewing needs
of energy viscerally generated
out of misguided
perception of male virility

Heart is a squeaky wheel
screeching loudest for a drop of oil,
a shot of deference all its own

Can you hear it?

It's the unintelligible squawk
akin to that of the mynah
so sincere and equally opaque
more often than not

Then again I was nothing but a
dumb kid with little knowledge of heart
too smart for his own good
and to this day remain so in many ways

But one thing's for sure,
win lose or draw
I stand for every draft I write

Luckily for me
heart caught wisdom on the backstretch and
never looked back

Thud

flaming out
so exhausted
can't sew a tired yarn
historically never an impediment
only a hurdle
for flight of fancy in rapid descent,
buckshot diplomacy
clips wings already bound,
a phoenix falls to earth
lands tangled among
vines & squiggly lines,
answers never heard
to questions never asked
best to stay put, rest

flaming out
bit by bit
hypnotized
lobotomized
marginalized
un-exorcised
un-synchronized,
struggling from grasp unyielding
of no discernible feature
aside from ubiquity

flaming out
a peanut gallery ran out of legumes
(the stage sighs relief)
trekking a journey of no end but one,
unsure of the logic
though logic landed me here to start,
few will lament
a typer gone missing among hordes
of missing typers

flaming out
unforeseen non-sequitur
no longer presents itself for remediation
dying kindling watches
as it flies by
uninterested any longer
like a cat
wise enough to see futility
chasing birds
arthritic bones won't oblige

flaming out
relationships sow seed of destruction
expectations unmet
psyche attacked
incapable of straight face when met
with honest representation
of straight mirror
in round world
exacerbating apex and valley undulation
he who doeth protest too much takes the wheel
though knows little of navigation

flaming out
a hole
bottom dwelling embers steal precious oxygen
from one another,
stand incredulous of progression impugned,
waxing nonsensical
wars of bastardized word unheard
mortars pierce airwaves
concertina wire surrounds media homes
perforated wings hold a final party
in a gilded house as
streets break under weight of
misguided repairmen
hired from Maytag Job Placement Dept.

recently nationalized

flaming out
burnt to a crisp
muse begs for salve
aloe for burns,
nothing to offer but a backstroke
and promise
that she'll cook as I cook
everything well done
some might say
black as charcoal heart
I just figure
we've got fire for a reason

flaming out
one more phoenix down
spent
ambivalent if not
apathetic, and if not for
requisite energy forever lost,
sociopathic,
thud
another phoenix alit,
muse-pilot burning in deafening silence,
a river overflows its banks
resting from a recently completed run,
a quill wind-drifts unattended
dripping red ink
searching for home
finding none

thud

Fire

flame passes serpentine tongue
smoke billows from flared nostril

can you smell dragon's breath?

what of breaths
emanating in bowels
beneath urban centers

do you taste brine
washed ashore
lapping sands with gentle taps
sea-birds fly in hunt

does the poor man seem noble or ig
the wealthy rich or lacking
in twisted distinctions of existence
that seem so senseless

do you feel the futility of
that question
laying beneath questions
when all toes snap to
overwhelming forces lacking decency
even for the truly pathetic
social strata dances fast when shots fall
at its feet of dusty sands

night blooming jasmine blossoms aromatic
perhaps those are the scents
you most readily detect

repulsed or aroused in guilt
tell the truth
which stand you

when man falls man
spraying Monty Python
from fractured septum

pitiful helplessness sleeps on a park bench
sits quietly
when not aroused by cop or other rogue
waits for the inevitable
dies of terminal hope for due haste

do you see human in eyes
buried in collages of all mosaics of
pain in a cold world
too great to conquer or do you
stand as jury
as to self determination
on one hand
while chastising success with diesel fire
on the other

do Libyan government attacks on dissidents
scavenging for food in filth camps
sicken you to no end
as you attempt to pound Amendment 2 to insignificance
are you that slow

can you smell any difference
between the laden and empty
when both are freshly shaven
and shod with like footwear

sun stars sky
winds mountains seas
lea grassland
stagnant flat mesa
rich gifted
poor unskilled

bejeweled as a princess
tattered as a pauper

hawks see not numbers
but a meal when hungry

doves seem to do more counting
sums just don't matter
even for snow white winged love
of empty belly

pride or prejudice
love or hate
malevolence or magnanimity
which influence you when writing yours
nobody stands higher than truth
sits above sin
especially he who would lay claim to such

human tongue splits to reptilian
fiery embers drop from sky
fall upon a lap not always willing
but ever able to bleed ink

smelling it all, touching and hearing
seeing and feeling
she decides where I go and she's not pure
insistent though
her truth will be exsanguinated or flame-spit
and her muse has a forked tongue
unfortunately enough venom for two lifetimes
though occasionally
he finds enough moments to smell antidote too
sulfur depletes as well
at least on occasion but is it just me or do
stockpiles seem to be
building

Escape from DC; A Semi Lucid Fractured Rant on Fracture

a rooster crows at midnight as the eagle lands
though the rooster has a cough and
eagles are harder to find than they once were
taking to tree tops to avoid capture
their days are numbered they so well know
the hounds are out and closing in

the coyotes watch as the wolves watch the vultures watch the
  hawks
watch the eagles as they alit
obscured against the grey sky, the raven watches all of them
  watching
all of them watch each other

reason has become a four letter word of six letters
though visceral reception of empathetic leaning had long lived
  in shadow
equipoise retains elusive properties I can't grasp

the prowlers are on the prowl prepping to loose battle cries
upon all perceived trespassers
though a stoned and fractured bunch they most clearly are

dazed and confused and stoned and trying to wage war
between the New Hawaii 5-0 and trips to 7-11 for ammunition
for empty food magazines as the Twilight Zone Marathon draws
  closer

the fire blazes outside their own door
a ship drowning in frigid sea
volcanoes blowing their lids for good
empires made artificially
bigger
as natural selection works to render them
smaller

the funeral pyre burns
the fiddle plays
yes in Rome
once more
and the band
yes the band goes on
as water overtakes the bow
but too outside your door, today,
the tide rises
the smoke billows
can't you hear the shrieking
smell the noxious fume of dying industry
and the bodies roasting with it

can't you see it in the prisons
a free country run by fear unions
human zoos to maintain corrupt status quo
all in the name of fright for those most avoid anyway

brought to you by those you'd eschew if you saw beneath their
  patches
at the cost of the freedom that allows you to divide via color
  lines
though you don't believe in division you say and
there's a good chance you've been
color blind from the start

your relativism has gotten the better of you
rendered you a hypocrite in your judgment of fellow man
and here on the edge of rebellion you remain fractured for you
  still
swallow their lies like a porn star swallows a money shot, trying
  to look elated

and it's here I'll sit pounding out my nonsense
as it seems more conducive to my ends than pounding a skull

though certainly far less efficient in effect
and most definitely lacking the instant gratification I learned
grabbing a toy from a box of Sugar-Smacks

yet, my magazines will remain full   of ammo,
and unwavering
yeah and maybe I'll toss in a Slurpee while I'm out
sweet smoke will rise from hemp paper
and coffee will course my veins
bleeding my guts

and the only cages I'd build would involve a town called DC
bordered by mines and copious electrified concertina wire
maybe someone should write a screenplay
then again, I think it's been done
actually I know it has - twice
we've escaped NY & LA
DC's rough though

funny, the bad guys wore white hats in those first two too
you knew better though, right?

Lotsa Luck

I walked down by the ocean after finishing the first of today's
  business,
under clear night skies of diamond stars,
in an aisle of last night's nuptials, I chose one seat to sit alone,
only my thoughts and playlist du jour
to distract me from the lonely picture that captured my
  thoughts.

An arbor, white, temporary
beneath sits a single chair,
behind, only infinity of sea,
boundless galaxy above.

Something struck me
a single chair under a fragile arbor
the only white
to be found is in what had happened
last night, assuming
it actually deserved virginal hue;
tomorrow promises
wither with each fresh breath.

It's the way of things
and as all that is today life shall tomorrow too pass,
so does it transcend
that lives grown together also
tend to die together.

Trying to stand up to
vagaries of simple existence as one,
it's a tough gig but
not as tough as it becomes when
the egg cracks
as most seem preordained to do.

Leaving a fragile arbor broken and
one chair at the table to soak up all the blood
in a fountain of forever questions
like what happened and where'd we go wrong.

The easy part is over.
I wish them luck.

Oneloa

in Pele's embrace
'neath shadows hers
cotton candy sand
soft cool kisses flow
channeled through
kiawe thickets wooden spiked paths
land upon necks
as nascent sky arises
        blue dotted puffy white
        birds chirp
        feral felines listen
oxygenated lifeblood
of native spirit
diffuses
blessing he who stands before
Kanaloa's garden blue
gazing far
yet seeing so little
mass incalculable
ebb and flow
tide's rapture

tapping blissful a' shore
tapping blissful a' soul

She Falls Silent When Most Sentient

a pile of autumn leaves lays in a stream
pre dusk sunsparks break through branch
      in perfect symmetry,
        of a full palette
captured for digital eternity

a small child glistens as his mother

though something it seems,
weighs in her powder blue seas
      belying the beauty
        and intoxicating smile
          a fire no doubt rages beneath

a darkness underlies
even the brightest of her paints

pristine forest appears to pine
in the frame of her lens

only in embrace of her precious brood
does her anchor lose focus
as clouds expelled leave naked joy
in the hue of baby blue

introspection seems branded upon her beauty
or perhaps I'm just projecting my own weakness

she falls silent when most sentient

seems to be some of that going around of late,
while for others a bullhorn fails to soothe

word spoken is often word rued

yet self immolate, we persist
lest our vaults of treasure
turn seed of implosion
or so it feels as ink
flows via IV like
warfarin blood
through paper
veins

perhaps it's better to be of fewer words to regret
in her eyes though, a different story

then again, I could just be projecting once more
I am prone to redundant behavior

Spilled Milk

there's a kid eating shoe leather somewhere
he musta spilled some milk or stolen some pills
not like there's much of a difference anyway

for his future he sees only away
distant canyons but a few miles as the crow flies

a pallet running of color into congealed
pools of blood
that taken and that shed
boots stick to
adhesion of bodily extract
extracted with
no regard as to cost to
either body or soul
not much difference
here either

like stolen pills
or maybe spilled milk
fluid runs equal
blood drops or busted nut
it all drains into
gutters already sopping
a quivering line
in sands a hefty cab fare
from virgin

overwhelmed streets of kids needing it
the buzzzz
freedom, a place to hide in plain sight
under bright lights
of the darkest of all darkness is where
you'll find them

and him, in a few years after he's eaten
his last leather
flips the bird to the metal flaked hills
to saner lands
infested with profound insanity

at least though
there's a difference between spilled milk
and stolen pills

one kills slowly as milk is rare in the cold
the other gets you killed certain
regardless at least your soul can remain
if you can keep it together and
remember the lessons learned at home
nobody loves you, trust yourself

stars shining bright are but illusory and likely dead
by the time they're seen
straps of internalized rage turned upon the loved
scar forever, no matter
lovely eastern reflections on consciousness

they've got it dropped down an octave to science now
stars today rotate
when dead in life or career or in Malibu recovery centers
they just change lights
disposable as guttermuck, even the brightest

what does that leave
cold huddled masses of no representation
keeping each other

but never turning their backs even on friends
loved ones yield keloid memory

what about that glass of milk

was so utterly important anyway, just askin'
oh and you never ran out of
your chemical romances despite my sticky fingers
so what was it about the milk again?

Another Lesson Learned

"Don't trust anybody. Nobody here will do you right."
-first street kid I ran into in Hollywood...

a runaway just taking a break
from dark of Hollywood streets
14 years of wide aging eyes

a squat- of sorts anyway
in Newhall we sat around a mirror
really just a table for a game of quarters

nihilist without a cause
always stirring up some shit
checks sometimes my ass couldn't cash

discussion turns to god
like rounding a corner and walking
face first into brick wall of unpleasant disposition

a fist smashes the mirror-table
in defense of god from my atheism
flies an unforgiving corner of jagged frisbee

county fire arrives
a bloody 2am scene in the making
what's your name son?

nihilist *with* a cause   *(not facing the 'rents*
I can't tell you just bandage me up
I'll be on my way

nose split open an inch and half
gash millimeters from left eye and blood careening off chin
all choice in the matter removed

nihilist without a cause mummy wrapped
can I have a smoke?
a resounding no heard from the crowd

Henry Mayo Newhall Hospital
over what seemed just gnarly laceration
after all the mirror was busted

er doc chastises youthful indiscretion
along with choice of hour for interrupting her day
getting my face smashed in god's name

nihilist without a cause
shut up old lady and do your thing
that I will insolent one but first parental release

trapped as a coyote
chewing off an arm not an option
waiting in angst

in luck uncle shows up
none too happy but a far better option
than he of my paternity

soon enough I'd face him
50 stitches and a smoke (thanks uncle) later
this wasn't gonna be pretty

in the house narcissism built
think the wound spared a worse fate
sitting before them in body yet of mind distant

finding myself adrift amongst
an amalgam of disparate thought though
of some thematic commonality

weighing the world with a child's scale-

is a nihilist with a cause still a nihilist or just a confused
   anarchist?
is a nihilist without a cause a redundancy?

philosophical esoterica an odd obsession
for distant youth of acute apatheia;
a vault no blow could penetrate however

blood drips flavor of death on tongue
trying for a nose breath through gauze gag
coughing up result of the favored excuse, free-will granted

shoulders slumped exhausted
a tirade escaped in theoretical machination   *(magic carpet*
   of choice
seeing lips move hearing not

remembering the lesson
that nobody would do me right
I sneak off incredulous

shaking my head
knowing once and for all
no one up there had my back

and to none would I bow

They Only Have Eyes For Two

they stride down alleys
as two lovers
dancing the last waltz

skies melt
atop electric Christmas trees
sneaker strung ornaments
swaying within snow drifts of
Santa Ana dust clouds

plastic tumbleweeds pass
frenzied spasms high low

cellophane curtains shimmer
reveal silhouette
shrinking growing shrinking growing

flat color sparkles metallic
in the dark of hypnosis

staring straight through window pane at all
nothing animated stares straight back
but lights trailing near and far

walls of blue drip red signature
on a line in death's guestbook
found splayed among whore job ads
in puddles of reflective glue
beneath feet of lovers
dancing the last waltz
for the last time- again

white pedals
fall from dove feet
turned gray

muted as inner voice
passing unheeded in wind

amidst adhesive of self reflection
sprayed as caustic mace
tears suffice for raindrops
melting walls of coroner's bounty
under strung-up high tops
strung out doves
dumpsters beating pulse of
piss stench alley
of cum stain pavement-

-twinkle eyes of two lovers
looking through pane
seeing but each other's cartoon

love via eyes gilded
with a layer of innocence
never recovered

blissful is apathy broken
by lovers' gaze-
blind to all but the gaze

even in gutters
under glimmering stars

dancing
the last waltz
one final time
again

Mercy Killing

Poems are hiding from me
I know they are
they pop up relentlessly
like cold sores
then, sure as they arrive,
they depart, individually forgotten,
like cold sores.

The cold is never gone,
sores remain in perpetuity
driven by a tankful of word,
lacking catalytic convertibility

I know they're still there.

They're alive in desperate eye
reflected in a lake of hardened tear
found on blank page, crushed
as wrecked cars
seated as a heap of broken dream
awaiting a final mercy killing.

Dead Stars are Heavy

wanting only to want
a clear flight path
over land trivia once
proclaimed its own

too many looks into the sun
serves as a stare at its antipode
too much light as the abyss
stare into either, both glare back

don't look up
stare not at the sun
eschew the wishes upon
stars which died long ago anyway

a head cocked rear
accommodating eyes staring up
leads to back pain
a vice-grip of
weight of achievement
left unachieved
and of that never begun
due to senses
gone numb to touch,
degraded blind
when a bit of sight
would help

spelunking caves best explored
with company
kinda like scuba buddy rules
as applied
to internal caverns of stalactites
questionable
in fortitude, limited in life expectancy

staring down
upon me and mine as spears prepping for
launch or plunge
as seems the more likely outcome
in current status

just wouldn't be fair
taking someone on this trip
those stalactites
oh those crazy stalactites
vindictive they are

no chance they let me off
nope, they're keeping me here to
watch exploration partners
fall to petrified mineral death
of dusty old books
demanding daily recognition
in a disheveled cave
under a bamboo cane cabana
of that used to whip
recalcitrant out of Singapore,
and a roof of
a Damoclean tragedy looming

calcified anger
awaiting a fresh victim

eyes fixated on that dark light
found on the brightest of days
during the loneliest of hours,
those I savor with all mine, yeah
but it makes sense to me

when all shares equal weight
balance is lost
contrary to popular misconception

it's long overdue
an adjustment that is
only I've yet
to find a chiropractor
that can handle
my girth of conflicted soul

stuck on land
looking out over sea
gazing into the galaxy, moonlit
wanting to want to look up again, but
hoping for a better set of stars to wish upon

my lawyer says it like this,
dead stars are excessively heavy
proper technique
should be followed when lifting

Country Bear Jamboree Growl

Owl eyes see much
so much that much of it isn't there
except when it is- laughing;
wise isn't always

Arms stretch tear snap
from sockets tired of working
bearing weight of heart
soul pumping reps of gray

A tug of gut-war
pits honest reflection
    (read: catch-22
paranoia its counterpoise
    (silicon its crime partner

All above a net of tangled web
of stagnant gray matter
as branch & vine hijack swamp

Twisted shadows bounce
off dancing shallows
never staying long enough
for even deft hands
to reach for a proper handshake

Instead they bound leap swirl
but don't stop for long
protecting the secret that is mine

Even from me
one turbulent jetty
removed from myself

Like a load of laundry

hot out of the dryer
clean but for the
stains chaining
you to their
trespass

If only whites and colors
separated themselves to reveal
apparitions in clarity for their disposal
rather than linger like images seated in your lap
while departing the haunted house searching for levity
found amid a bunch of country bears playing banjos somewhere
never to be discovered as anvils of age forge ahead in bellows of
smoke

How Many Boulders To The Margins

overburdened privilege
to target in the margins
to predator
eating what's killed
punching holes through the 10 ring
center page
dead right brain returns to life
most sure gun misfires
instructions went dyslexic
ready fire aim
aging
settling into a tremble
I shoot a group of right angles
pulled low and left
on a target round as round gets
clean holes
center page
satisfy no longer
rather weigh in truth
looking back down
to get high
if pipe dreams birth
the hunt's crippled enough
too much
oh to be back in
invisible ink
surrounding the 10 ring noise
back in the margins
though no longer a target
just living
eating that presented when
the clock strikes
now

Six Ways to Sunday

stars look west for sleep
eastern rays appear
despite my protestations

where light, I seek dark

a tree awakens before my eyes
tangled branches reveal nothing warm

elusive peace of mind
hides among a morass of branch and leaf

each limb a stop at
déjà vu corner
an intersection of
echo and now

out of sight is out of mind
sometimes it's best that way

challenged minds
don't do their owners in
overthinking

with night- the capacity to ignore,
enjoy respite
a skill woefully absent my DNA
fitting as an elegy perhaps

as he arrived, so too has he departed

peak and valley rhythm
isn't rhythm at all
white men can't dance

an EEG runs flat-line
guess that's light out, isn't it
tomorrow just got easy

rest in lieu of the fight

a journey objectively old
takes on all comers
maybe its time for numb

a 'Y' juncture in the road
with signs, lot of 'em
all point six ways to Sunday

A Stroll Down Sentiment Row

In febrile haste,
Gloom falls to earth
desperately seeking Doom.

Gloom is a blue sort,
typically moody of disposition,
in search of the same.

Once alit,
it takes no time
Doom is everywhere.
Gloom is beside himself with joy.

Misery loves company
replete with vast caches thereof,
Humanity is only too
happy to share for Humanity is
sometimes Misery
looking for the likes of Gloom
for a bit of small talk.

With each look into each eye,
Eastern mystic
or Western pragmatic,
Gloom sees Doom if looking
closely enough, seeing past the façade,
the uncomfortable creature comfort.

There is a corner in every eye
reserved for Doom
and Gloom for that matter,
     after all
        they are Siamese twins,
but from that corner, tears fall
if you let them

they're coming eventually, like it
or not.

There's time and place for all,
defines balance frankly
yet what a fucked up redundancy,
Gloom & Doom
when one would serve just fine.
What to tell the angels, outnumbered two to one?

My Brain Crashed Into Two Poems & Can't Get Up

(With a nod (at least & again) to Mark Hartenbach)

warped vision fronting warped mind
mangles perception
well maybe not if shape is all in the
eye of the beholder
unfortunately trees fall in forests even
when nobody's hearing
still however stormy days survived seem to
teach that sums greater than
those of ubiquitous equation of
multiple variable
actually take the field
when that which is seen
storms from locker-room in
logical construction but
for the ability to cross streets
without adult supervision
among keloid tissue of that not visible in
a mind blocked by
tangled groves of geometry
leading to webs of
differentiation and re-integration
sticky as fly paper to
conceptualization of greener pastures of
right side tilt found at
three o'clock from cognition's vantage point
tortured artists have nothing on
bludgeoned souls of logic
creativity yet unborn from shells too thick
but cognizant that Pythagoras
didn't quite explain it all
as devil in detail
hijacks angel of viscera
everybody knows everything

nobody gets anything

Ain't Nothing Sacred Anymore

stuck in an electrified channel
a lexicon devil knew he lost
his battle with demons which
died right where they birthed
self hate piercing black ovum

staring into echoes of childhood tear ducts gone arid
puff passes in a purple cloud now and in all veracity
doesn't really care about that kid whatever his name
likely at a law firm screwing the last dragon anyway
so who the fuck needs that fair-weathered puke brat

mary had her lamb before going on the lam
her incestuous father had chops that night
it was the better of alternatives but she really did
love that little lamb almost as much as daddy did
his favorite little girl soon to be the crowd pleaser

trouble at the north pole is expected this year
blitzen got blitzed on too many blintzes and
rudolph is in betty ford though workers are
endeavoring tirelessly to get him off her and
back into his holding corral 'til he sobers up

your old man eats the cookies anyway
so the fat man is boycotting just your house
if he finds two replacement reindeer
sands drip fast, they don't train overnight
and the elves are prepping a strike

I employ all resources to comprehend the incomprehensible only
to find truth in fallacy for in line with multiplication tables come
lesson plans for lambs, sleighs and fat pederasts clad in red suits
which parenthetically should be a warning and if it isn't true that
little boy blew why did I buy all your monotheistic dogma

anyhow

I've got a date with an old dragon buddy of mine
sure he will spew smoke at first, ah sweet smoke
he'll get over it soon enough, we'll laugh aloud
up until he breaks out that old mirrored stone
truth reveals in age and often unfortunately so

wonder if he ever met that lexicon dude
think they might have gotten along well
but then again I am a blind man signing
with deaf finger anything but dexterous
schooled on dragons as eyes longed far

quite far from post war box classroom

Day Dreaming Away (For A. Razor)

adrift on a sampan
aimlessly afloat on a lake named Dahl
replete with odd life
of odd names lost in ash of age,
weight of existence

a pterodactyl passes above, nonchalant
rendering an Escher shadow
upon gentle ripple of chocolate current

a curious wave gliding gently
'tween red rock and black sand candy
tropical palm and desert scrub
emptying not in sea but hearts, minds
made too old too young

tick tock a keyboard strikes, running loose
guided only by boundless galaxy
found under tipsy boulders
where imagination grows free among fern
and it need make no sense

unicorns love fern
perhaps that's why they're among the more popular
of valley residents

thank whatever is holy
they didn't fall to the white rifle
as the Loompa

left unattended, lichen moss and fern overpopulate
leaving a bitter aftertaste in the ground-chocolate river table
clearly nothing one would tend to take lightly
impossible to miss is biological detritus weighing on soul

besides what other use for the white protuberance
if not to till soil for progeny to sow, should
the reaper leave something to reap

perhaps of no added value
but infinity of fantasy unimpeded

 as the suns give way to the moons
the big dipper takes a big dip
> *(he got bigger with the sweets*
> *though I'm not sure it's germane*
just a pinch between the cheek and gum
plenty of juice to spit on sinners

you know the guy
locked in shackles of reason
a prisoner of his own war

unable
to taste the sweet fog
elate soaring above prehistory on a magic carpet
or nurture the inner child as shadowy echo silences laughter

I know him also
all too well and he'll pay
sinning in the name of knowledge
when inner child is being candy-bombed by magic drones

magic drones which never should have lost supremacy
to a bunch of stats lessons and dogma ingested over generations
taught by unforgiving deities basking in their own-ness, casting
  lightning on
right brains desperate for outlet from leftist prison as crayons
  seek children of all age;

each and every child covered in finger paint and pudding
Schoolhouse Rock, Dr. Seuss and Shel Silverstein

Time To Smoke This Joint, Smokey (For Scott Wannberg)

A Storm Cloud walked into a bar
Medusa ordered a warm toddy to heat up
serpentine guardians not at
work today as they mourn the loss of Riff
She better get used to their ennui and quick…
Riff saw beneath Medusa's scourge
he had a special place for maligned serpents
knew it wasn't their fault their boss was a bitch.

Hell's a hell of a place to hang,
worse if the cat's got your tongue and just
lost his ninth life to travel high
the fang gone, states go into fugue.

Lonely snakes have a shitty time
warming up to task
Toothless, left to hiss in futility,
scream in rage.
No, really.
Scream in rage against the Machine
before you bless it
but make sure you
do
bless the Machine
sure it's cold and dank
and occasionally needs a hug, but from
Depravity's deepest holes,
and we all know just how deep her holes are,
from them,
a voice
a heart,
bled in ink till the chickens came home
to Roost-er…tarty chicks,
they just love his roast, man could he cook.

The Pearly Gates open wide
they have a new guest
never one for elitism, he asks
if he can just hang in
the lobby for a little while longer,
check out the scene, dig?

"Not Good Enough lost his job as court jester,"
was the reply.

It's Now or Never, a band he never dug, currently on loop,
the other residents are up in arms   and a few legs
his presence is requested immediately.

"Why do you think we sent for you?"
"Cause you know not of what I speak of course."

"No matter.
You can hear the trumpets can't you?"
"Yep, clear as a cataract."
"No matter Riff, you're on."

"Well ok, just don't make me play in the Bushes
they give me a rash."

The Gorgon is soon to be all gone
her serpents are done with stone masonry
master of their mantra flew the coop
taking the strike out of them; they just up and quit
or down and quit as the case so may be,
but really it's an uptick too long in the tooth, us
lowly reptilians tire as man.

Hey, I feel something
tear pour from above, washing
balderdash in acid rain.

Looks like he found his way to Court to Jest,
certainly they're tears of laughter guffawed by
the very gods being insulted for their inhumanity.

Metaphor is lost on them however and in their
grand egos, the big boys
pat each other on the back as the new Jester
casts barbed hooks
their arrogance can never fathom.

Perhaps, if he were less prolific, he'd
still be here suffering with the rest of the huddled mass
of confusion through which he wove word like a
an Olympian attacking the giant slalom.

With all us snakes downstairs opting out like
a French Poodle from a German liaison
		not very....well...successfully,
a few neighbors are bound to get Riffed
if they're Raff.

Sunday's may fool some of the people
some of the time
but never Riff, who, on the other hand,
could fool all of the gods
all of the time.

Good luck to them, falling from their thrones
in throes of laughter at quivers of acerbic arrows
aimed in honed perfection right where
their hearts should be.

"It's time to smoke this joint, Smokey," a voice
was heard from the back row,
"Flame isn't the sole purview of they on the acmes
which sit now at your feet."

RIP Scott Wannberg

Skid Row L.A.

cracked pavement mattress
  too firm for most
holding bodies once possessing souls
  lost to eternity
victims of gene and circumstance
  ill in the head
    if not yet then soon
strangled by a constrictor named success
mugged by addiction
forgotten in shadow of towering granite
soaked in reek
infested with parasites
riddled with sickness
  delivered by cold
dropped in sewers to fend for incapacitated selves
  by hospitals offering no hospice
landfilled flesh supplied by neighboring agencies
  dedicated to protect and serve
self medicated by fortified wine and sizzling rock
tossed to wolves
  by unrepentant egg and sperm donors
discarded into margins
perpetually pushed further across tracks
  of thinning acreage
increasingly more desolate lands
  where trains sleep and wake
    thousand yard stares blink their last
  in paramedic truck strobe
    or crosshairs of sector car spotlight
    or developer's project
helicopters circle as cowboys tending herd
  where all talent is wasted
    any remains scrawled on walls and dumpsters
  appreciated never
    drowning in a sea of appliance box tents

  condom wrappers
    infected syringes
   crack vial lids
    newsprint tumbleweed
   miscreants of bad intent
    hair-scab blood pools
jack booted thugs practice thuggery
  who's to tell anyway
    no iPhone cameras here
humanity forgotten
  until an eyesore develops
    blocking gentrified view
   demanding ophthalmological action
copters return
  riding humans like Texas doggies
indigent exodus east
  pace commensurate with each for sale sign
   on parcels no longer suitable for even a train's sleep
blood spills as resource dries to none
base survival instinct clobbers weakness to its knees
  knights of night in search of prey
granite marble and crystal growing at
  febrile pace unsustainable
   dot gilded skyline
    ever more distant
  though jobs falter
east increasingly unwelcoming
  west grew hostile years ago
a trash compactor created
  pressing more excrement from
    society's bowels
vacancy strikes even that of ivory construct
  sunlight passes empty office floors
strikes coffee vendor
  receptionist
    executive alike
Mad Dog sales spike

   with each failure
families falter
   with each non-existent paycheck
another potential cast-off
    relegated to kinetic reality of
      fetid air
shrunken refugee camps
    squeezed farther from civilization
   whatever that means
    when no civility exists
   when marginalization grows
    as marginal land is buried
   under granite stone and marble
    as it all once was
   as it likely will be again
the constrictor's stranglehold tightens
   little remains to constrict
no palm trees to look pretty
zombies enter a mission
   occasionally a person exits
    recognizable as such
   by reflection of light off what's left
desert wanderers on grounds unfriendly
   grasping the last of human dignity
    with depleted grip
   and a faint glint of life
    found in a dying gaze
   struggling to hold on
hoping to fail

playing like copeland when moon is called for

in search of word
a dog chasing its tail
gods sweeping their fails

nearing collapse
exhaustion takes a drug test
finds it's not pure

though inconclusive results
reveal high grade fatigue
coursing weathered vessels

channels blocked
fingers take vacation
land in arthritic keystrokes

cracking up ain't all it's cracked up to be
rubber walls call my name
I don't respond

not that it would be an inconvenience
but for inability to conceive adequate retort
capable of surviving to full term

visceral necessity meets temporal incapacity
resulting in a duel of no winner
both seem to be losing once prodigious aim

pondering all under the stars
towering redwood to rippling ocean blue
superglue keeps tongue from cat

unarticulated calculations cripple
perhaps tongue grabbing cats are less culpable
than synapses frozen in isolation

phrasing lost in violent wind weighs heavy
sugar coated iron plates
placed uneven on opposing barbell sleeves

mass rests on a
fulcrum directly above
heart soon to rupture

vanished forever in deterioration
second derivative of depletion gone parabolic
a nasty case of vertigo shows up

manifest destiny
soon meets a flame suffocating
wick approaches wax

mute bands of speechless agony
dare try to escape pre-demential prison
synaptic breaks repel the attempt

she ain't talking
'cept in archaic dialect unintelligible
but for redundant theme

word drifts across stunted cerebral mass
unnoticed
but for blank space unintended as such

leaving empty graves
dusty rugs not well beaten
so in need of beating

A Matter of Price

in a fetid swamp of vast treasure
festering sores won't heal
a porn shop opens its doors

low rent style for low rent types
in low rent neighborhoods getting pricier
opposed to high end joints in
places already high rent and gentrified
where girls start with starlit eyes
under spells of a sign high upon a hill

a few may find their way up gilded heights
mostly they end in low lying beds of black roses
not unlike those of the working stiffs who
cum stiff in and on them in pre-civilization savagery
under spells of nature
likely not found in opaque tunnel vision relativism

don't seek chivalry in
hard-ons of he of
smarmy Cheshire tooth
none will be found

don't search for doors
into souls sold cheap
they open to brick
which often crumbles
before your eyes

the stains remain in perpetuity
no shower
can cleanse dying willows
in the soul of a little girl smart enough
to know she's little but a whore
zip-code notwithstanding

wonder if she might feel better
were she to learn that so are the rest of us
it's all a matter of price, isn't it?

Assorted Contemplations of a Stranger in a Strange Animal Farm

meditating
on a lonely tor
our house is glass
hostage to our own sin
sweat pours down naked skin
blindfolded ball-gagged bound tight
open wounds bleeding red rivers unimpeded
cattle branded MIA despite my negative sentiment
towards labels separating me from the universe at large
I am quite capable of burning popular bridges solo
a series of numbers represents our existence
collective puzzles of academic muck
cohesion poor but for base dna
prisoners of our own war
our house is glass
I throw rocks
in futility

popular moral conviction pops infected eardrums
slithering blobs of molten metal hate sear
divisive discord cuts like fine cutlery
a dime has two sides barely apart
apart is a relative term where
borders are breached daily
obliging a word other
than asymptotic
which just is
no longer
accurate
no longer
the panacea
spray & pray
the new normal
there's no friendly fire

for there are no more friends
killing for cause leaves wounded
relax said the pig *all animals are equal*
some are more equal than others although
as long as its consensus principle can drop dead

Blurring Lines in the Abstract of a Linear Mind

entropy
abject chaos
overtakes overwhelmed
new world order gone mad
not in use sign indicates some
waking from wet dreams sopping
nightmare wolf dons dream sheep garb
fooling most although most are quite easily conned
the sky has fallen below sea level rendering all questions valid
knowing it's illusory but nevertheless no longer pointing up
  proclaiming sky
ground beneath collapsing arches begs description as being up
pleas met by deaf ears though I must cop to intrigue
pythagoras nailed it but my lines curve
nietzsche crushed it but backward
war rages across hemispheres
blood rivers flow black ink
from order comes hasty
abject chaos
entropy

Dark

loquacious drowned in a weeklong downpour of four decades
monosyllabic motivates for its debut
word takes a flight of fancy to illumination found only in dark
cave-bound stands in proud virtue

abyss is but light focused on
undesirable visage seen in
broken rain puddle reflection

carpe diem assumes a homonym meaning in another tongue
seizing day all day every day
binding miscreant missives to masturbatory machination
never done jerking itself off

gratification evades reach
escapes out the window with happy ending
which never reaches climax

antiquated aspiration fell to bottom wrung of ladder
its shins scrape to bare bone
overwhelming clotted river which dictates course
though it failed map reading

successive waves of undulating cognitive rhythm crash overhead
ubiquitous reminders of unpleasant demeanor
not fit for prime time though quite apt for a cave-dwelling ogre

On the Tip of Tongue Yet Inarticulable

my tongue's tied with some advanced sailing knot
out of which I'm unable to slither
sliding in and out, under and over have been core
to my survival ever since ever

devoid of alternative means of remediation
it's all I can do but reach for
cold steel forever found in my right pocket

kept opposite that of open vein
spilling black,
no heed to stain left for all to see

a blade has gone dull as its possessor
modern kevlar line doesn't readily oblige
to even honed blade of laceration regardless

perhaps I need find peace with the rope
a substitute form of communication
when voice goes silent and signing seems
a bit optimistic given bound hands

searching the depths of all I've ever known
I once again find a means
by which to slice myself free for the moment

my shadow will soon again catch me off guard
its harder and harder cutting free of the sails as winds
turn acrid, water black and current drags me old before my time

guess I shoulda paid more attention in cub scouts
perhaps cub scouts shoulda paid more attention to me
semantics notwithstanding I can't untie a knot to save my
  fucking life
yet somehow fashioning a noose around my own neck presents
  little if any difficulty

Deviant New Normal of the So Called All-Inclusive

a mirage rises from fresh tar
evokes ghostly images
none of which are believable

but for their manifestation before us
open eyes don't equate to sight
trash cans offer but don't implore use

word sits
screams silently
unread

cult of personality
has overtaken culture
usurped reason

past foibles forgotten in echo silenced
usurped by perception
a blindfold of malodorous conception

mirrors have been painted black
likeness too graphic for all audiences
best to stick with secular cliché

piss rolls down my leg
they say it's raining cats and dogs
I see only the excretions

no doubt we tempt fate
walk on hot coals
yet must pray for faith

a devil in angel wings
cult of personality
a new deviant normal

running on an empty tank
hiding from truth
a nod to holier than thou

umbrage to non-extant glimmer
rising off sun drenched pavement
revealing truth all spot but few can see

Outcast

outer reaches of playgrounds serving as oases of contemplation
where swirling sadness contrasts smiles of judgmental peers
unaware of pain or simply offloading various degrees of
transgression perpetrated from storm drains clogged with
invective of masses incapable of understanding
he who understands not himself juxtaposed against a world
spinning off its axis in a backwards march circumnavigating a
sun offering no solace

cast out upon deranged protoplasmic creatures once resembling
human now shadows of trespasses executed at their own
hands and those of other reflective of genetics gone haywire
exacerbated by nurturing arms of no warmth
even in the embrace of heat rivaling stifling conditions of
tropical bird aviaries where the rainbow shines its healing
glow through skylights upon fluttering wings complete in
representation of all hues of the palette and possessing no
enemies to fear

alone in perpetual discovery of the vicissitudes of existence
where no path lay clear and friends are but puff adders donning
stripes of zebras bearing promises of unicorns which never come
true for there's yet to be a confirmed sighting of horned horses
though the world we call ours is still in its juvenile stages and
hope remains for their appearance however the viper's strike is
lightning and rarely seen until too late and toxins permanently
impair the few unlucky survivors of its own terrified reaction

signs of sudden dysfunctional home syndrome are breaking the
charts with a bullet strategically aimed at the heart of the matter
which is another way of saying we're running low on kevlar
whose efficacy versus ten ring shots to adolescent soul remains
in question as adhd is prominently displayed to eyes receptive to
bright hues of diabetic triggering cereal boxes and sub-cerebral
hemorrhaging of free will to the vagaries of hormonal imbalance

exemplified by a toucan escaped from the aforementioned aviary

backed up into a vertex of a wall between two adjoining buildings seeking anonymity lodged among cruelties of childhood and utter desperation of maturity crippled in fear of rejection by a universe not revolving around all suns then eventually realizing despite growling retorts and uninformed conjecture that love is indefinable and solitude doesn't necessarily indicate loneliness long underrated rather opportunity for reflection of a life possibly worth living but the jury is out on philosophical diatribe of a life unexamined

the playground has grown old and fallen in disrepair yet when in use resembles nothing remotely similar to that which fostered much extrapolation and little fascination as lesser minds and greater weights burdened the spurned excluded incapable of letting the world go despite an inability to change a fucking thing in the scope of things as eight year old outcast or pugilist of four decades in search of reason where none exists and finally squiggles where lines stand in formation and unicorns romp across grassy leaves in the sky

Dorothy & Toto

I've been known to attract some shit from time to time
not exactly sure why (inner voice: he's lying)
just is what it is I guess
rarely if ever does it end
with a simple fuck you.

I open at cocksucker
raise me an asshole and I'll re-raise
-douchebag
'til I'm all in with all I got
and I got.

Problem is everybody's so worried of
what everybody else may believe
we've brought upon ourselves
pox of black and white donut-gestapo justice
on that rightfully fit for a civil court
in a tort action if it's fit for discussion at all,
via regulation of the worst intention-
to silence truth, however ugly
decide decency in subjective ambiguity
what constitutes arrestable hate
as opposed to that the masses accept
in the land of the free individual.

For me- a dilemma of epic proportions
cuz if we're in it
I'm coming for you where it hurts
quite probably slinging
that cocksucker ante into the pot
like Nolan Ryan on cortisone day
for if you raise my ire, I'll lash at
your guts in blank numb dumb.

So there was this guy

really one and a half X's to be honest
an ex-writer too, no pun intended,
nobody seemed to care much for
anything he had to say anymore
he lived at bare sustenance level
figured I'd be friendly to him and
his stupid little dog too...um I mean
special little dog, though I'm not sure
I can say that any more either
fuck I'm confused.

He'd seen better days
so I did mine to be cordial
and of course, no good deed goes...

Trying to be decent, I pet his dog
asked a stupid question
let him think I actually cared of the answer
of course, no good deed goes...

Responding with venom
he actually assaulted my query
proffered cuz I knew the world
had passed him by and flipped
the bird as it strode low
in the Benz he derided while
truly wishing he too so traveled.

There was a reason the world no longer cared
-he was no longer relevant.

So it's Venice on Washington Blvd
half block from the pier
local coffee shop catered to cops
-free coffee so we all know where five-o
would go for their joe unfortunately
three jurisdictions falling on top of my space

turning the little shop into a virtual
tactical operations center
LAPD, Sheriff's & Culver City PD
men standing tall in numbers
though less so in stature than once
guns on hips
badges adorning chest
radios, always radios, yes
for if six cops are already too many
why not a baker's dozen for good measure?

Anyway, one thing led to another,
rather than fall to a pool of vomit left by
excessively inebriated coeds
who had one too many after their first
Dorothy pulled an ace from his sleeve, dialed 911
yelled "Cop!" like a homie smacks 'Domino Motherfucker'
and went all in
leaving me with nothing but word
and a new name for this
asshole and his little dog Toto too.

Not willing to stand on my head
in county for a weekend over this shit
I resorted to my final parting bet
threw down hard
"Fuck you, you douchebag motherfucking
 cocksucker," oops...

Apparently I just committed a hate crime
according to the new law of the land
or so he shouted to 911
and me for that matter, standing yards away
as I had separated his corpse
from my demons of unforgiving retribution
but of what was I accused?

Clearly "Fuck you," is hateful
fuck it, we're all under arrest then
'cept he/she yet to so utter
like I said, we're all under arrest.

Motherfucking?
I doubt he ever did for one
secondly I don't hate motherfuckers
I am one, all around
I rather enjoy fucking mothers myself
can't be it.

Douchebag?
I for one am grateful for the creation
besides it's an inanimate object
guess it's a nasty word
when well applied
but seriously
can I not just hate the cans, Jerk?

Suppose that just leaves cocksucker
may be your thing, ain't mine
but hey, vanilla and chocolate all around in America
and as mentioned, cocksucker or not, it IS my ante
odd though, of all spoken in the speed of Tourette, cocksucker
stood as the least hateful of all for I was simply speaking truth
he was a cocksucker
figuratively and literally
of the literal I harbor no ill will
vanilla and chocolate, remember
but of the figurative, I harbor no sympathy
can't call a cocksucker a cocksucker, in the US of A?

Fuck me!

Careful of that for which you wish
when regulating human interaction

you will undoubtedly accomplish
exactly what you set out to avoid
unless yours is filling up courts
housing humans like monkeys
in zoos not fit for zoo monkeys.

All you get is an already slippery slope
plowed higher, closer to avalanche at
a moment's notice or wailing of siren.

Interpretation and misunderstanding ensue
I want my enemies loud and clear before me
not festering hate beneath the surface for fear
of arrest or omission from the next cocktail party
I'd at least give mine that courtesy...a soap box...
unadulterated truth.

You may just find that in your poorly intentioned good
    intentions
you breed more hate than you can possibly comprehend
simply by outlawing it...well then again, the war on drugs is
    working
prohibition prohibition how we love you prohibition
something's gotta create jobs and keep control over the populace
I hear religion's gone fishing, guess we'll need new law!

Bubbles tenuous in nature tend to pop
bubbles so tenuous in nature as to prevent copless discord?
well they tend to pop absolutely...
absolutely terribly.

So Dorothy, fuck you
your little dog Toto too
and your cop muscles.

Ahh, I feel better already.

Fog

fog approaches
deep dark
menacing
indecipherable
a vague blur
foreboding
but indecipherable
clear days have gone extinct
even where amber luminescence
casts its brightest glow
where pearly whites are pearl
chewing on insanity
considering its integrity
what's of this fog
portentous
neither white nor black
gray
as existence skews linear sustenance
rendering future of no clarity
but for transparency of that known
death and taxes
and a opaque threatening fog
drawing me towards its ends
heavy as an anvil precariously placed
serious as a stalker of wicked intent
or perhaps a field of harmless daisies
in a world of harm
a magnet pulling me into the light
either way
its nothing more than a projection
rays cracking through a brick wall
growth turns to wither
or a phoenix rises
climbing vertical
abyss averted

the clouds are gray
then again perhaps I'm extrapolating
a forecast not to be trusted

Hopped a Bus

Grabbed an old RTD on Ventura
heading from privileged boredom to
din and bright light of decay,
the most magnificent urban depletion
creator of ultimate character, human and edificial
home to the most charming of hordes
lacking all,
but mostly dignity
not to be found for 990 miles of
thousand yard stares.

But for here under gilded skies
a moon reflected shadow read 'Hollywood'
and it was here they resided,
lacking any compulsion to explain circumstance
for theirs was no different
in ends than those of other filthy beaten rugs whose dust,
visible in the air plain as day
fell to pavement as a bloodied recipient of a 40 oz. greeting.

Times have changed, but you can still
taste it
as you pass alleys cum urinals,
see it
in the few honest eyes remaining,
smell it
in the well worn, poorly washed being,
feel it
in blood stuck to your boots as you stroll away.

Further out they go as success breeds failure
among those already failed
in search of new range in land of gentrification,
however it was what it was,
is what it is, and I preferred what was, honest,

to what has become, a clean whore,
where streetwalkers are no longer welcome, but
conventions and award ceremonies are big business, and Sheen
is deified, especially for clean whores; decry
corporate America you may but your whore now takes Amex,
don't leave home without it.

Yeah, well that wasn't then…yet
I saw past purview of myopic binocular
to a world seemingly so much more appealing
through kaleidoscope eye of four-way window pane,
knew just where to find it and found it, the Sunset 440 Motel-
  then
don't ask me what it is- now, I'm too fried to know,
soon there would be no more bus rides to score the sacred paper,
ground underfoot would become bed, but for then,
just a stop on a four tab trip from lawns manicured to perfection
to simmering stars, melting cops, burning suburbs
and charred remnants of pre-baby boom lifecycle gone awry.

Depraved Reflection

orange fire soon to rise
illuminating new world order
quite long out of order

mighty sea current flows determined
trawling for redemption
presenting a coupon years expired

day light strikes fear
shining upon sin unimaginable
yet patently undeniable

moon rise, save us our soul
staring into mirrors of depraved reflection
begging dark, deserving none

Rent a Cop High Wire Near Miss

try as I will
you just won't let me be

judge this cover once more if you dare
find lies beneath cliché you will
dermal images take life
scepters fly free

trust me here hear me here
as I tire
of petty judgment cast
debilitate
from myopic visions
set upon me by lesser eyes
    ((look at me when I talk to you- dig?))
of bulbs fading
dim to dimmer to dimmest
to withered
in garden beds demolished
by waffle sole
of simple brand print:

TREAD CAREFULLY
Kihei/LA

next time colors you'll hear sounds you'll see
ask "Me, oh why me?"   when you wake

trust me here hear me here
si me busces me encuentras
you don't want that

book covers tear
reveal truth you can't handle

skull cracks as eggshell
some books are best judged by their covers
or just left the fuck alone

feel me?

Odoratio Suetes

a familiar odor travels with the winds
fires rage in pits echoing of embers passed
water main remains rusted and dry
hordes gather to celebrate individual independence
wealthy anachronisms fund history
progeny perfectly prepped to prove it repeats
berkeley took a hard right turn
dove wings are plastered over east bay wolves
droogs predictably carry automatics
opportunistic meek inherit a league of liana
world falls to no common sense
a rose garden in winter is littered with petals
a familiar odor passes in the wind

Rage

searing heat rises from boiling feet
lost on a journey never to end until
there's no more ever at hand

destination unknown though a mirage
of goal posts looms faint in the smudged distance
on a map strongly resembling a pretzel

inability to come upon sufficient release
for dissonant thought creates more of the same
battle of dichotomous rumination not soon to relent

precise snipers with precise rifles despite their chaotic rounds
of mass popular invective
train sights on a body mass lacking body armor
popping rounds into wilting self perception

Bukowski chimes in, spitting his piece
reminding the peaceful of their propensity for violence
and superlative marksmanship skill

questions of worth begin talking to each other
branding themselves on a spirit
unsure from the start of its weight on the sell out scale

bloated from the never ending journey
lower limbs carry on at all hours, unable to meditate when somewhere
in shadow must be a worthy punching bag

Disconnected

a leaf off its branch
ripped by storm from a trunk,
itself uprooted

an arm excised at the shoulder
separated by a thousand miles

telephonic contact gone silent
lines split in the land of self absorption
sometimes its simply easier

a lizard king lost his tail
whiles days away pondering the question
certain he prefers less weight

  that equilibrium stems from tail is fable
   a fairy tale designed to dam tears of children
  youngsters holding broken reptilian protuberances

unaware of the lizard's relief
all too cognizant of his pain

Sunset Dance With Buddy Guy & Suicidal Tendencies

Sitting under a gently swaying palm
watching day turn to night
in a dance on a floor of no boundary
but for the horizon

One might think all is well
espying me watching flickering light
like eyes fighting sleep
futilely pushing back against the dark

Suicidal strings race from chord to chord
fermented barley and hops chase wisps of anesthetic smoke
and medicine cabinet sutures
one might think all is well but the western front is besieged

The floor has fallen from beneath feet of
tapping tides, rendering an eve of flame thrower potency
as held in the hands of original passion
in new wrapping, enveloping sanity in a slam pit found only at
  night

One Way Out

anemic choking demons
pecked relentless on regulatory binds
trapping their virtue

free none too soon they dance
precarious high wire tangos
over net of hot ember

left blissfully blind in free warm light
they breathe deep, puke fossilized carbon

white wings exited too
they do travel as one-

white & black wings
acrimony no matter,
walk hand in hand

lobbing firebombs
darkness seals fate

scorched earth erases days
clocks can't tick backwards
but for within ink heartbeats

white hope douses flame in piss
drips rivulets of civility on mass conflagration
confounded by its own abject futility

balance-seeking peace
as worthy journey
is just too much stress

a million death needles
where choice never ends

an open pine box
sets to shut a lifetime

a baby nears birth
slap, cry

awaiting bail in a cell
I grin ear to ear
 choice no longer mine
there is no going back

behind bars I'm free
fat fem aria sung,
I'm finally free

Red Pool

two
things rule
all mankind
fear and greed

that
which courses
tremors of fright
beacons of light

different
for every man
though common threads
are common

craving
is another word
for greed of imminent need
in perception

sometimes
nothing else will do

shiny happy people crowd objects
think they're above that bestowed by nature
some misguided attempt at civilization
where none exists   Darwin be damned

I crave not acceptance of masses
I care not of misnomers spelled 'society'
today I have a taste for something
blood   same as every day

yet today it's yours I plan to spill
all the condemnation

conjured under the sun and moon
mean nothing, nothing else will do

no vampiric machination
only a congealed pool
of your syphilitic river
fills my vision   red
 today you will bleed
this I assure you
deal with it
or don't   I crave blood

your blood
with all my greed
all my temporary acrimonious insanity
and no fear whatsoever

Personality

battles rage inside
sybil speaks gibberish
another county heard from
discomfort is prevailing wisdom
a war is two people in the same room
maybe it's heart cracking to two chambers
divisive constant flux writing history
painting electrified intermediates
deafening voices to others
blinding singular light
in abyss of oneself

On an Unlit Street

hide me from light
I don't want to see
don't wanna be seen
beyond my icy glare

I want to sense
to embrace naked death
as a welcome room-mate
no longer the mother of all
fears, but the salve
of all ills

no longer the phantom on the cold floor
beneath the bed
but the one that lay beside me in warmth

let darkness envelope
skies and streets and buildings
and again make me feel safe
out of the light
out of their sight
outta my own

make lightness of day go far away
run amok of me, it has
bring the reaper to my shoulder
so I can laugh at his silhouette

let people of day return home
leave streets safe for the unsafe
open its door to me; let me in
transport me to the precipice
so that I may stomp a heavy soul
again; lose the weight that splits

take me to the motherfucking end
wrestle me at the cliff's edge
higher than the highest peaks
dare me to look over the brim
of the steepest slope over the
darkest abyss and
dare me to stare
right into its motherfucking eye
while it stares right the fuck back

Seeking What's Lost Where I Fear No Evil

neck-deep in the valley of no return
a search party seeks innocence not to be found
innocent is another way of saying purity yet to be tested
everything has its price and purity is part and parcel of
 everything
a diamond in the rough can be no more than polish worn to its
 jaded foundation
although it could be argued that the scales of justice are
 weighted against the living
rendering all subject to abrasion of sanders extant simply to
 fractionalize self
waters part yet exodus is exhausted and red sea drips on worn
 sole
though I thought I heard a herd of feral humans splashing
futility permeates noxious air of looming ends
a haitian necktie flames in the distance

One Choice
(inspired by Angry Samoans)

stampeding rhythm drives adolescent hormonal entropy
no outlet but for rage
easing eyes gone way too old way too young

an iron plate resides
weighs deep within thorax
crushes heart

renders shoulders a' slope
eyes between apathy and death
when not contemplating yours

a cloud sits gray
surrounds my space
invading soul already jonesing bad
for a bit of vitamin d
visible at a distance rarely but
rarely visible at all

begging for a spot
a packed gym stands silent

teachers, peers alike
bring but more pressure where need is not
the iron's gaining weight
Jenny Craig's nowhere to be found
Gold's is out shooting dec

smoke billows but only the like can see
and the like split first chance they had

red protest screams unimpeded
tied to a stake
a brand scorches future

present died years ago

split, I can but bail
my old man's a fatso
there's no doubt
who owns this house

burning anvils remind
he who might otherwise forget

Slow Drain

shotguns end all discussion
philistine philosophers ponder pondering
answers blow in the wind

a strange feeling washes over me
not a feeling so much as raging river
the salmon are all dead

invasive species have choked out life
no time to tap out
ref calls an end due to utter paralysis

staring at while standing atop glistening white sand
which always seems to stare back
walking through a maze of options with no choices

vultures circle overhead
carrion visages in their prognostic view
awaiting final breath

saccharine dreams result in cavities
craters too deep
even for egress of mythical protoavis

grounded in quicksand
searching for a root or vine or joint
anything fixed upon which to claim purchase

a shotgun would end the discussion though
philistine philosophers will always ponder pondering
and the answers will blow in dismal winds of overwhelming
  dissonance

Solitaire

a cacophony of cascading correlations plays poker upstairs
no regard for maudlin propriety is offered though would likely
   be declined anyway
grabbing a chair at the table seems preordained yet unhealthy
not that unhealthy has ever stopped me before and frankly I'm
   beyond giving a fuck
introductions to life affirming are met with angry boulders
though it's been suggested the author of my Sisyphean trauma
   bleeds my own name
which shouldn't suggest an attempt at self immolation
but fact lacking implication of failed tries at auto-destruction at
   which I never fail
proven by ash at feet scented predictably of seared flesh
smoke swirls about a cranial suture on the verge of coming
   unglued at any moment
ripped at the seams courtesy of intransigent thought run amok
which like drawing breath is no more than an indication that I
   awoke this morning
a dynamic of a lifetime's worth of what for enters the room
begging immediate retort to questions of no answer asked in
   machine gun staccato
antes fall as cards are dealt from the bottom of the deck
as flaming sarsens occupy Wall Street from atop torso near
   imminent collapse
a river of nonsensical non sequiturs waxes redundant
the table spontaneously combusts leaving but a lone wolf and
   pack of cards one short
a partial deck making for a maddening game of solitaire
a battle of wits with the poorly armed as the train labeled
   unanswerable chugs closer
delivering a fresh batch of incendiary what ifs for kindling
just in case the world is in fact flat and extant woodsheds go up
   in electric flame
in case the check raiser gets re-raised by a man resembling jesus
and of greatest importance the correlations begin arguing

themselves into oblivion
ordering scotch and soda, tossing 'em back like jello shot
 youngsters
but everybody knows parasitic correlations hate oblivion despite
 irony they'll never get
so in truth the only one I'm fooling is myself and even I don't
 buy it

The Last of the New Mohicans…

1983. The last of the Mohicans was dying off at the blood lust of related but dichotomous descent. Tribal warfare among urban and suburban MIA. Rhythmic flow of chaos emptied. In its wake depleted stock of the heart of an era. My only escape escaping to another world. Hopefully better. Hope is the purview of the foolish. And those who know not why they carry on but do so nonetheless. Perhaps because they still hope. An interesting paradox for he without faith and genetically challenged with hyper-analytical predilections. I remain unsure as into which group of fools I fall.

Sunset Blvd. Hollywood Hills Motel. About half way between the Sunset 440, home to the purple pyramid palace of turn on tune in drop out and the Seventh Veil. Home to nude chickens. Themselves half way between horrible childhood and miserable existence yet to be experienced. Hawks circled above and around . Businessmen, urchins and lurkers alike laying out bucks for a peek at the end zone of lust before such field trips got written off on T&E reports. Before high end ass vendors lined the margins of high end neighborhoods.

Panhandled a few bucks. Pitched in. Got a space on the floor to crash. A shower. For a night or two anyway. Learned trust. As in no one. Five ten or twenty of the last tribe of Mohawk Nation lined different spots in a hierarchy of time served. Forty ounces of anger passed around until the soldier died arid. Then another. Death is the purview of soldiers. All kinds. Many fell there. Many punctures opened channels for plungers to ease pain. In turn causing more. Live fast die young not just a mantra shouted by Keith Morris but a prediction.

Across from my corner of floor, Johnny whose hair formed an edge eight inches high stretching in the grip of Aqua Net Extra Super Hold. Forehead to collar. Banging away on a little birdie from Los Feliz slumming it. Cute. Petite. Young.

Blonde. Sweet actually. Pretended not to notice though my hard on was throbbing through the reality. I had a thing for this particular little finch though was far down the food chain. FNG. Just had to deal with it. Yeah, and I was in no position talk neighborhoods. That from which I ran looked like paradise from airplane windows. Nice from far. Far from nice if caught in the wrong cage. Gilded mountains stood proud in the distance. Some of us knew the truth upon which they were built. Nothing like the lies they told us.

Standing tall above me, my first test. Buzz. Big dude. Talking some shit. I slept through it. Until I awoke to it. "Poser," was a common dis. "He looks like he's just a kid. Give him a break." A welcome refrain from the chromosomal dos equis. He relented. I couldn't take him one on one. Not yet. My scissors stayed holstered. Sheathed in a torn pocket of hard ridden jeans. Right rear. Always right rear. To this day. The real poser sang King of Pain in perfect harmony with Sting on the cheap tv/radio the next morning. Buzz. Poser. A lone set of minor chords doesn't punk rock make. Fuck you.

In the bed a liberty spiked, overly pierced asshole. Seventeen years of garbage on two legs. Couldn't tell you where he came from. Knew not the anvil he lugged upon his shoulders. Hence won't judge but to say he was an always testing you fuck. First name Bobby. If you knew him, you know the rest. Seemed to be ring leader of the circus. Ergo, the bed. Downstairs, Ramon, peddling his wares while tending a couple of lost daughters. Or forgotten. Or kicked to the curb. Either way, Ramon didn't suffer. Had a chance to take me off. Didn't. Good enough for me. Assorted friends and talk behind their backs when they left types moving in and out like bees scurrying through a hive.

Tripping through the streets. Looking for new squats to keep from the death stench of cramped motel space. Church brown bag lunches on Highland. Tuesdays I think. Many years have since been buried. Maybe it was Tuesday and Thursday. Who knows. A hot meal once a week from another house of a god I never bought into. Though empathy is a virtue. Faithful or otherwise.

Fires razed the old sweat lodges. The motel took to the winds as did the Canterbury on Cherokee. The winds fueled more centripetal sucking of yet more of the old dilapidated charming into a vortex of gentrified new and polished. Lifeless but for pompous zombies unaware of their mortality, their blood thirst and their wallets. What remained was walking dead. And gasping edifices yet to realize their looming extinction. But what of the outcast? The kicked out. Kicked on. Food for larceny and larcenous brutes alike? Where would they venture? The last of the Mohicans. Seattle it would seem. Aqua Net sales plummet.

Stoned Grumblings from a Rock in the Pacific

hangin' at one am with Hank III
an empty lot in a small industrial park
fluorescent lights about 50 feet apart
illuminate an 8x11 blank canvas begging for warmth
two pit bull mixes pass, stopping
momentarily as if rent-a-cops walking their beat
checking out the dude with the bike sitting with a blank canvas
begging for warmth
a third mutt gallops spastic as if called to assist
but late to the party
something about the latter pulls
heart strings strum for the third wheel
seemingly left out of festivities
like a kid perpetually on the outside
an inner circle unwelcoming
and unwelcome, never seeing light
as there's always a circumference a bit smaller
one in which theirs just won't fit
and on them, this weighs
the canvas begins to take on texture-warming
I blow hot air on icicles
an actual security guard approaches
as if alerted by the k-9 passersby
checks to see if I'm ok
fuck, I must be a long way from Kansas, Toto
it's what I got
guess everything can't be confrontation
I know, sad
easy to lose sight of that fact however
as people want more and more from other people
with no more to give
as war decimates life and landscape alike
as hereditary hatred
mates with that of nurture genesis
creating...hatred, more hatred

as intractable greed for the grand dream
equates to a house fire
a garage heavy of acquired weight
and so very light on equity
as history is sent to the wood shed
donning a ball-gag and straight jacket for good measure
as government has grown bigger
than the people
though it's not much of a surprise
the people ask for more
while rights drown in left field
and left field is as flooded as right
despite laughable protestations of asinine presumption
misconception bred of personal bias
a wet breeze presses a chill through the ticking clock
as Europe burns
tweakers hide in shadow
faint scent of salt is the only aroma to grace olfactory
I imagine pungent, noxious
air of urban deterioration 2200 miles northeast
transporting mind
where body isn't, penning as I pine
a different time and place loom quite large indeed
a fantasy of what is not
and never was
of no delusion that it will ever be
just a glimmer that maybe
should the stars align just perchance
one day
Hank and I will meet again
and finish this canvas
enveloped by the odor of life
found only where life
is bought and sold so cheap
where the pyre of winter trash cans
is all that illuminates
birth and death and all in between

as seen in cracked eyes
of the cracked
where David Allan Coe might meet
John Doe
where the third dog is often welcome
going by a name, a quiet name
but a name not a number
where my heart longs to find itself
missing so many years
a hostage of four decades
a callous resembling a .45 caliber barrel
mars temporal skin
perhaps it's time to release myself or
in the spirit of Mr. Brooks,
back off or the atheist-jew gets it

Time's Changing 5

Boris left. Off to the land of I don't fucking know. The whale's mouth just closed. I have no torch. Glad that binary solitaire still throws cards at me. What else to do with fidgety digits? Still spiraling down greased rails. Twenty two ounces of where am I mixed with a burning bush smelling nothing like it did the first time and a handful of this will make you better. Trust me. I have a degree. A chaser of adolescent anger music on the rocks with a Leonard Cohen twist. Still blind though I've contracted an intimidating wobble. Approach with caution.

A shooting star downed by missile defense. The plunger fills with blood on my orders. I'm gonna be sick. Twenty angels die as toxic tide brings agony to an end. I killed my best friend. Gonna be sick. Any more barbs in that bag Doc? Maybe a couple of dilaudid. Take the edge off. Someone could get hurt. Someone is devastated. Medicated into who are you standing in front of my mirror. The old days found the fountain of youth. Their stare pierces my walking corpse like a dagger through a thorax with a four chamber vacancy.

Two wheels split lanes. How does a motorcycle get so fucked up? Right grip sinks to higher speeds. Might be time to reconsider closing left brain doors. Approaching my own land of I don't fucking know. It's 50/50 if I maintain un-control over this beast. Scraping steel on wet turns. Something someone grab the bars. There's hay and a warm sleeping spot in the garage. Live to fight another day. Key word fight. Running a gauntlet of falling rocks. Searching for a pry bar for that whale's mouth. Does anybody have a fucking lantern? Please?

Sun sets on a life filled with so much 'why' I cannot comprehend magnitude of its loss. A fire of orange and red burning through ominous cumulus clouds. Demanding appropriate respect for the smallest creature of the greatest substance. Like a Mike Taylor poem. Another deal struck on my behalf without my knowledge though I'd have gladly accepted. Not ratified at the crossroads but on far off shores of another plane. An ominous tenebrous gray send off looms in distance immeasurable to all but fate. Ok by me. Just take care of my friend. Carry him off in warm wind. Heal his wounds. Let him chase lizards again. He'll only off a couple. Repair his impaired renal function. Give him a cave. A place all his own to sleep off days spent traipsing grassy fields. Sharpen his claws and give him a trim. He's had a long trip. Make him a kitten again.

Dragons as far as the eye can see. A few left to slay. Gotta get to work. Hourglass denominator is getting heavy. Tipsy. Weebles sometimes fall. Dreaming impossible. Flying straight into a gaggle of geese. This motor fears not your honk. Don't care that the Hudson sits not below my wings. Nobody ever said the act couldn't be foolish. Why I treat foolhardy as anathema is left to be determined. Seems however the river needs to run upstream. Upending sandy time pieces. Soon. Prior to the work's finalization. No illusion of grassy fields nor meek prey to be found upon completion of this picture. Just a bus straight to hell. Or a Kardashian taping. Is there a difference? Either way I doubt my route will stray far on the y axis. Low is low. A fact to which I'm indifferent. But for the smallest creature of the greatest substance. Soar high Boris. Don't expect me anytime soon. Other than heaven shoots half a minute of angle out a mile yet has me in .50 caliber sights at twenty feet. Dead to rights. Have a field mouse for me. I hear they taste just like chicken.

seizure

sparks flicker though it's storming
word escapes
gibberish scribble
disjointed thought
   singing the same chorus
  singing in the rain   woeful melody
   repeatedly a gang rape of my skull
cognition gone incognito
I see pavement in front of me
observe birds nesting
feral cats hide in tall wheat grass
rumbling seas whitecap below
   stormy scene painted tar
  meaningless
   background to a painting not painted
all circuits out of order
motor lacks oil
lacrimal duct detached long ago
river locks need find keys
though blissful is inability to ponder
    what   may   come   to   pass
alit before me a red headed cardinal
perhaps they're all red headed
this one digging not for precious metal
looks like the sound in my head,
sounds like the colors of rainbow
sensory overload passes lightning
inkwells burst nonsense
the cat's dead and dog asleep
some things I recall
like the painful silence of muse
   as my head rips open
  singing the song of no lyric
   overstaying its welcome
like withdrawal

or lawyers and their bloated retainers,
bottles of solution solving nothing
a horse ran off with my voice
left me a frog as collateral
he croaked
a silent scream won't howl
I twist in the blustery squall
wonder when the minefield
might be cleared
if blooming star flowers
will ever die
leave me in my own winds
return my tongue
    before sparklers blister what remains
this is your brain on drugs
    now delivers oatmeal on a platter
this has been a public service announcement
    expect no service
wires crossed,
can't see past polychromatic convulsing sky,
bursting with energy I am unable to harness
taking the last train to clarksville
as pop rocks steal my thunder

Do They Know

all's not quiet on the western front
fabric of a life changing rapidly
knots mar the woven cloth
the kid's aren't alright
felony steals youth
old too soon appears
trains are leaving stations
boxcars screech innocence gone
corroded metal marks blind journey

sun will fall
moon will rise
tigers will attack

structures will develop
developments will pressure
displaced is suffering

no, all's not quiet on the western front
we're all that matters caught a cold
humility hits like a white shark
searing unknown brands gut
scarred esophagus burns
the eagle has landed too hard
nope, the kids are far from alright
the rooster never crowed at midnight
crap dice fly sorties over chips you drop

yes, the sun will fall
as the moon will rise
I wonder if even they
have a clue as to why

THE END

Danny Baker, a runaway at 14 from the facade of a gilded house in the hills above Los Angeles, has seen life from the gutters to the towers. A high-school dropout, he landed on Wall St. at 20 in a move that only served to add to the dissonance of a rebel mind constantly searching for a youth never experienced. Danny explores his conflict in dichotomous writes of both unflinching, sometimes brutal intensity and honest empathy for the human condition. Danny's work has been published in Paraphillia Magazine Vol. 11, The Examiner, The Edgar Allan Poet Library and The Nervous Breakdown. Danny is to be featured with ten other writers in Heliocentric Presses' soon to be released *Into the Valley of Hinnom: A Dark Poetry Anthology, Volume I* and is expected to appear shortly in Deep Tissue 16. He recently held his debut reading at Beyond Baroque. Currently residing on Maui, Danny, now 42, is working on several writing projects.

On FRACTURED by Danny Baker –

"Throughout these pages, filled with muscular spills of language, collisions of image, and emotion, I am filled with Danny Baker's sense of personal mission, no less than a social activism. Perhaps "there is no elixir" ('Corroded Eroded and Tired'), but these poems do more than tread a dance of no-hope. Each poem is a performance piece enacted in the reader's head, vividly calling the words into substance. FRACTURED is a must."

Carolyn Srygley-Moore, Author of *Memory Rituals: An Army of Suns, and Songs Scared from the Conch//as Voices Carry.*

"I have anxiously awaited this volume of poetry and have been pushing this poet for over a year to pound the pavement and find an editor that feels the pulse of the earth and the nature of man as he does. Danny Baker is multi dimensional; gifted in changing
gears in structure; and awakens the imagination; the inner poet in all of us. Read one piece of his poetry and you will be waiting for the next verse to fall from his pen."

Diana Rose, Poet, Editor of *The Weekly Top 12*, Book Reviewer

"danny baker is a force of nature. he eats stars then torches the pages. one of my favorite poets from the first time i read him"

mark hartenbach, Author of *Monster Poems and Appalachia Koans,* Editor at *Non Compos Mentis Press.*

★

"Danny Baker writes like a house on fire fueled with an inexhaustible passion for language. His words are a rage of poetic wonder, a journey into the soul of an artistic warrior."

S.A. Griffin, Editor *The Outlaw Bible of American Poetry*

www.ingramcontent.com/pod-product-compliance
Lightning Source LLC
Chambersburg PA
CBHW051653040426
42446CB00009B/1118